CAR CARE MADE EASY

ALEX MOSS

CAR CARE MADE EASY

DISCLAIMER

The publisher and author of this book have made every effort to be as accurate and complete as possible in the creation of the content within this book. However, neither party warrants or represents at any time that the contents within are accurate due to the rapidly changing nature of the automotive industry.

The publisher and author will not be responsible for any losses or damages of any kind incurred by the reader, whether directly or indirectly arising from the use of the information found within this book. The author and publisher reserve the right to make changes without notice. The publisher and author assume no responsibility or liability whatsoever on behalf of the reader of this book.

CONTENTS

GETTING STARTED

INTRODUCTION

Since first publishing Car Care Made Easy in 2010, a few things have changed. Perhaps most obviously, electric cars weren't really a thing. Nissan's Leaf, the first mainstream EV, didn't arrive until the following year, in 2011. There were a few hybrid cars roaming the roads, but even the Prius wasn't so common until Uber came along! EVs are now specifically covered in the book.

That said, many of the basics of owning and running a car haven't changed; servicing, insurance, road tax and MOTs for example. The same applies to the regular maintenance aspects of your car that need taking care of between services and MOTs. Cars still use brake fluid and coolant, blow fuses, get flat batteries and have four rubber doughnuts keeping them in contact with the road. Having a good grasp of the basics not only keeps you safe but will probably save you some money along the way too. Many of these checks are also part of the practical driving test in the UK, as the 'Show Me, Tell Me' questions.

This updated edition of Car Care Made Easy follows the same popular formula that's helped thousands of motorists for over a decade and gathered so many five-star reviews. Inside you'll find invaluable background knowledge, advice on what to buy and easy to follow step-by-step guides taking you through simple checks that will keep your car in tip-top condition.

Car Care Made Easy still remains a jargon free zone! Some car care books aimed at beginners are littered with mechanic speak, which defeats the point. Jargon has either been binned or is clearly explained where necessary. You also won't need a set of spanners to do any of the jobs in this book.

So, whether you're just starting out on your driving journey, or have been behind the wheel for many years, Car Care Made Easy is your guide to being better under the bonnet and beyond!

Thanks for buying a copy of this book; I wish you safe and happy motoring.

Alex

USING THIS BOOK
STEP-BY-STEP KEY

All the step-by-step guides in this book tell you exactly what you'll need to do a job. For example, if a funnel is useful to avoid spills or you should wear rubber gloves to protect your skin. Most of the symbols should be self-explanatory, however, you can always refer to the key below if you're not sure.

GENERAL ITEMS

Rubber Gloves

Kitchen Roll

Funnel

Level Ground

Tap Water

Torch

FLUIDS & SPARES

Engine Oil

Coolant

Brake Fluid

Steering Fluid

Screenwash

Spare Fuse

Spare Bulb

Spare Wheel

EQUIPMENT

Jump Start Pack

Jump Leads

Tread Gauge

Pressure Gauge

Tyre Inflator

Car Jack

Wheel Brace

ELECTRIC VEHICLES: Some sections of the book will only apply to cars with an Internal Combustion Engine (you'll sometimes hear this referred to as ICE) i.e. vehicles that run on petrol or diesel. Where a section is unlikely to apply to an electric vehicle, such as checking engine oil, it's marked with the following symbol. Do check your owners handbook to be completely sure, as there are some anomalies out there!

OPEN THE BONNET

(1) FIND BONNET RELEASE

Find the bonnet release lever inside the car and pull the handle.

The most common place to find it is the front footwell on the driver or passenger side.

(2) RELEASE BONNET CATCH

The bonnet will pop up slightly when you've pulled the handle inside the car. You'll now need to locate and release the safety catch under the bonnet.
(On some cars a small lever may pop through the grill instead.)

(3) RAISE BONNET

Hold the spring loaded safety catch open as you lift the bonnet. The bonnet may now lift and hold itself up. Alternatively you may have to fix it with a bonnet prop.

(4) FIX BONNET OPEN

If your car has a bonnet prop, lift the metal arm up and locate it into the slot at the edge of the bonnet. Once located, slide across and lock in place before letting go of the bonnet.

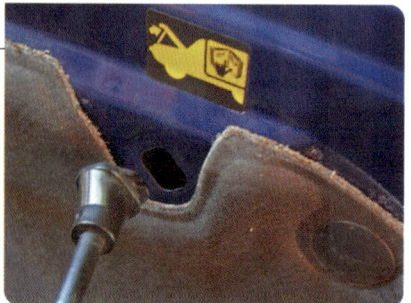

UNDER THE BONNET

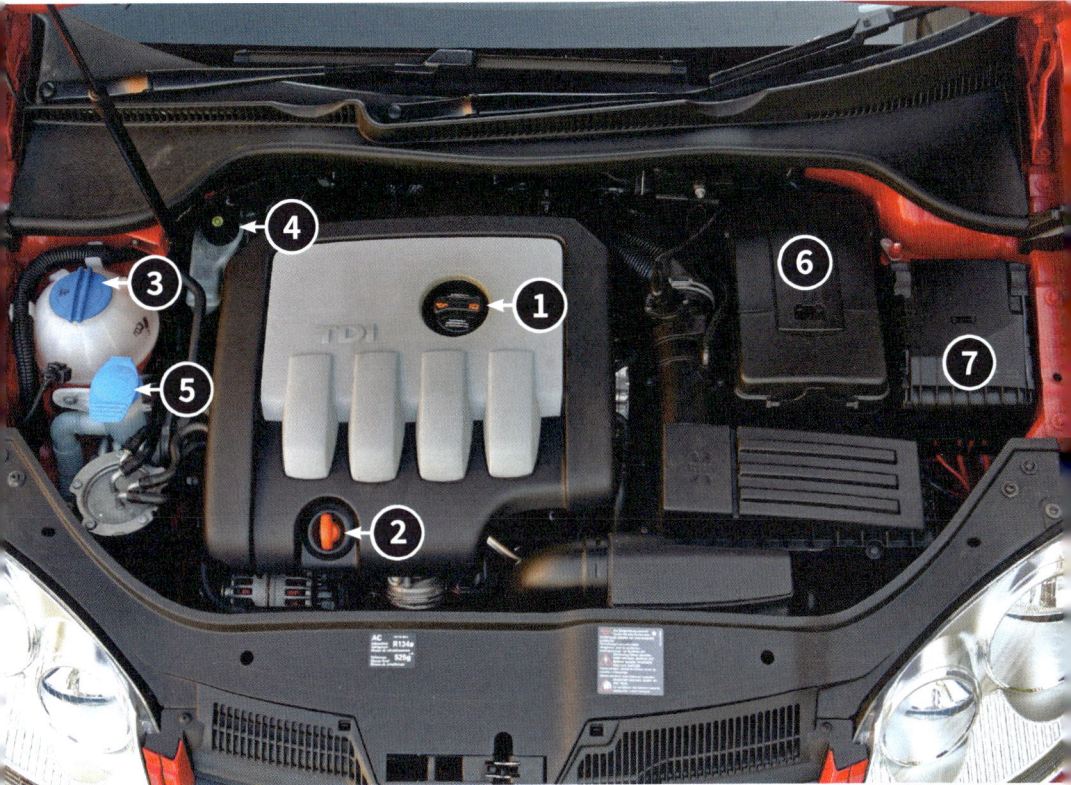

Although they might be in a different place, the key areas under the bonnet look very similar on every car. The next few pages will help you identify where everything is on yours. Electric vehicles will have less, for example, no oil filler cap or dipstick.

1. OIL FILLER CAP
2. OIL LEVEL DIPSTICK
3. COOLANT TANK
4. BRAKE FLUID RESERVOIR
5. SCREEN WASH BOTTLE
6. BATTERY
7. FUSE BOX

UNDER THE BONNET

① OIL FILLER CAP

If you've checked the oil level and it needs a top up, this is what you'll be looking for. It should have 'OIL' written on the cap or have a picture of a dripping can.

② OIL LEVEL DIPSTICK

The dipstick is used to check the oil level. The top of it is usually a yellow or orange hoop. When you pull the dipstick out, you'll see it's a long metal rod. At the end of this you will find the MIN and MAX marks.

③ COOLANT TANK

Most coolant tanks are made of clear plastic with MIN and MAX marks on the side. Never take off the cap if you've just driven the car as boiling coolant could spray out.

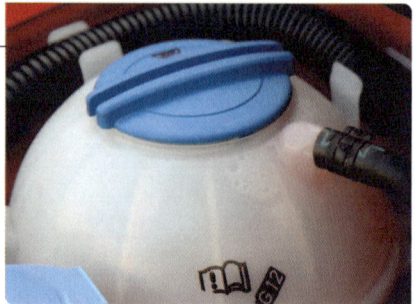

④ BRAKE FLUID RESERVOIR

The brake fluid reservoir is made of clear plastic and is smaller than the coolant tank. It's usually placed towards the back of the engine bay on the driver's side.

SCREEN WASH BOTTLE (5)

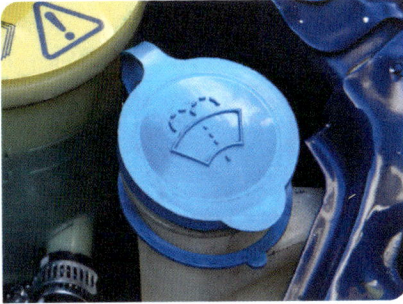

The washer bottle cap is generally blue and marked with a symbol like the one on the left. On some cars, a second washer bottle is fitted in the boot for the rear wiper.

BATTERY (6)

The battery is a large oblong with a positive terminal one end and negative the other. *(It's sometimes covered by a plastic lid.)* If you can't find it under the bonnet, it may be in the boot, possibly under the floor mat.

FUSEBOX (7)

The fuse box under the bonnet is normally covered by a plastic lid. These fuses are for high power circuits, such as the one used to start the car. You'll often have a second fuse box inside the car.

POWER STEERING BOTTLE (*)

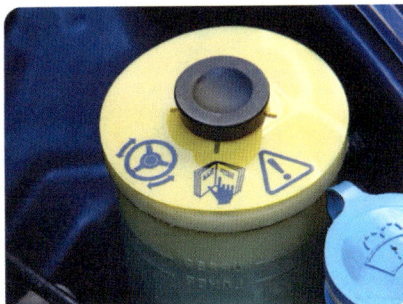

The power steering bottle is often made from semi-clear plastic and is commonly marked with a steering wheel symbol. In most modern cars the power steering is electric, so there will not be a fluid reservoir.

EV CAR CARE

BACKGROUND KNOWLEDGE

An electric vehicle (EV) generally requires less maintenance than a petrol or diesel vehicle. The number of moving parts in an internal combustion engine (ICE) can be well over 1000, whereas an EV may have less than 50. There is less to service and maintain, with no engine oil to change or top up. EVs generally only have three key fluids that need to be topped up regularly: coolant fluid, brake fluid and windscreen washer fluid, with few exceptions. Coolant is important for EVs, as it's used to regulate the battery temperature and other components, preventing overheating. (See the next page for more information and tips.)

Apart from engine oil and in most cases, power steering fluid, all other sections of this book apply to EVs. Just take particular note of the warnings around jump starting electric and hybrid vehicles. EV's and hybrids have two electrical systems; one low-voltage that's used to power things like the radio and lights, just like an ICE car. The other is the high-voltage system that powers the motor and drives the wheels. The low-voltage system (normally 12 volts) is the only one you may be able to jump-start using another vehicle's battery or with a portable jump starter. It's essential to follow the manufacturer's guidelines and instructions in your owner's manual before attempting to jump-start the 12-volt battery.

The bright orange cables you'll find under the bonnet of an EV are the high-voltage cables. They can carry anywhere between 300-800 volts or more. This is far higher than the 230v plug sockets in your home. Keep away from these!

EV BATTERY CARE

Whilst we're looking at EV Car Care, it makes sense to talk about battery care for electric vehicles. Here, we're talking about the high voltage battery, which can be called the 'traction battery' or 'drive battery'. This is because it provides the power to move the vehicle. The traction battery is a rechargeable pack that typically uses lithium-ion technology to store energy. It's designed to provide high voltage, high capacity, and high power output to the electric motors that drive the wheels. Like any battery, it degrades over time. In an electric car, this generally means the range of the car reduces as it gets older. However, there are certain things you can do to look after the traction battery. The following tips will help extend it's useful life.

Avoid frequent deep discharges: Lithium-ion batteries in EVs, degrade more quickly when they are frequently discharged to a low level. Avoid fully discharging your battery on a regular basis. Instead aim to keep the charge level between 20% and 80%.

Avoid extreme temperatures: High temperatures can accelerate battery degradation, so try to park your car in a cool and shaded area whenever possible. Similarly, extreme cold temperatures for extended periods of time can also negatively affect the battery.

Use regenerative braking: Regenerative braking puts power back into the battery when you lift off the accelerator. This helps reduce the overall load on the battery and increases driving range. In doing so, it reduces the number of charge cycles the battery undergoes.

Avoid fast charging too frequently: Fast charging, although convenient, can contribute to faster battery degradation. Try to avoid using fast charging too frequently. Instead aim to charge your vehicle at a slower rate whenever possible, like overnight at home.

Go steady: Rapid acceleration draws higher amounts of electrical current from the battery. This creates excess heat, which is bad for it and can put extra stress on the battery's structure. Avoid frequent rapid acceleration in order to extend the battery life of an EV.

ENGINE OIL

BACKGROUND KNOWLEDGE

Oil covers the moving metal parts of the engine with a thin film, allowing them to slip freely past each other. Think of it like adding oil to a hot pan; Without the oil, the food sticks to the pan and burns. Oil also helps keep the engine cool and cleans away the dirty deposits that are left behind when fuel is burnt.

Oil plays a vital role in determining the life span of an engine, so as well as being topped up it needs to be changed regularly or eventually it turns into a gloopy sludge. A filter is used to trap all the deposits collected by the oil and must be changed at the same time.

Oil only fully protects the engine when it's warmed up. Revving the car too hard in the first few miles of your journey will cause unnecessary wear and tear and shorten the life of the engine.

Although modern cars tend to use less oil than older ones, they still need checking regularly between services. The rate at which an engine uses oil will vary from car to car but some can use a litre or more in between servicing. If an engine gets low on oil it wears out faster and can also suffer from overheating problems. If left to run very low it may seize up altogether and leave you with a big bill for a new engine.

PISTON PROTECTOR

Inside your engine are pistons, which generate power when fuel combusts. They sit inside a metal jacket, known as a cylinder bore or in other words, the engine wall. The distance between the piston and the engine wall is often less than the width of a human hair. This is why engine oil is so essential. It forms a protective film that reduces friction, prevents wear, and ensures the engine operates smoothly and efficiently.

WHAT TO BUY

Engine oil comes in three main types; mineral, synthetic and semi synthetic. Most modern cars will use one of the latter two which are known as 'multi-grade' and means their thickness is different depending on the temperature. The oil is thinner when cold so when you first start the car it flows more easily and protects the engine faster.

The right oil for your car will depend on who it's made by, the engine size and whether it's petrol or diesel. For help finding the right oil, visit a motorspares website. Alternatively, check your car handbook or call a local dealership.

A multi-grade oil is shown by two numbers separated by a 'W' i.e. 5W-30. The '5' refers to the thickness when cold and the '30' is the thickness when hot. The lower the first number the thinner the oil is when cold, so a 5W-40 is thinner than a 10W-40. The higher the second number, the thicker the oil is when the car has warmed up.

"Oil usually comes in five litre or one litre containers. A smaller one litre bottle is ideal to keep in the boot for top-ups."

Can I just top up when the oil light comes on?

The oil warning light tells you there isn't enough oil to protect the engine so don't use it as your reminder to top up. Aim to give your oil level a quick check every other time you fill up with fuel.

CHECK YOUR
ENGINE OIL

When your car is switched off, the oil sits at the bottom of the engine in what is known as the 'sump'. When the car is running, oil gets pumped all around the engine, so you'll need to let the oil drop back down into the sump before trying to check the oil level. Leave the car to rest for at least five minutes after you switch it off and be careful what you touch as the engine will still be very hot.

Make sure the car is parked on level ground when checking the oil level or your reading will be inaccurate.

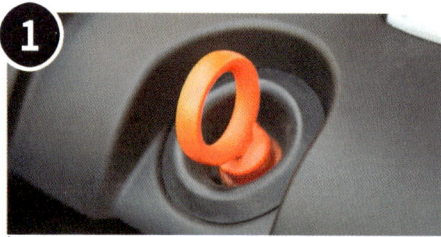

1

LOCATE DIPSTICK

Find the dipstick and remove it by pulling the handle, which is usually a yellow or orange hoop. On some cars it could be a black handle with 'OIL' or a dripping oil can marked on it.

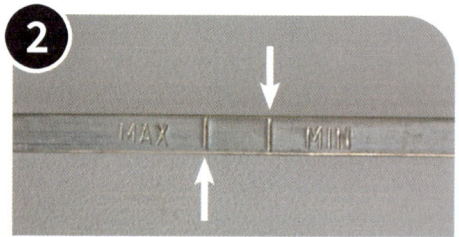

2

FIND MIN / MAX MARKS

Familiarise yourself with the MIN/MAX marks but don't try reading the level yet. Wipe the stick and push it all the way back into its tube.

3

CHECK LEVEL

Remove the dipstick again and this time take a look at the oil level. If it's below the half way mark you'll need to top up.

4

REPLACE DIPSTICK

Put the dipstick back once you've read the level.

TOP-UP YOUR
ENGINE OIL

Always top up bit-by-bit, than trying to get the level right in one go. Recheck the level on the dipstick after you've added some oil, remembering to give it at least 30 seconds to drop to the bottom of the engine. On most cars, the difference between the minimum and maximum marks on the dipstick is about one litre. If you overfill, the excess oil makes the engine work harder and use more fuel. The increased pressure on the engine can also result in oil leaks and damage to the catalytic converter. A tiny bit over the max mark probably won't be the end of the world, but if you go way over, don't risk damaging the engine by driving it. Some of the oil will need to be drained out first and you'll need the help of a breakdown service.

1

LOCATE OIL FILLER CAP

Find the oil filler cap and remove it. Use a cloth to help you get a better grip, as they can be tough to unscrew. Put the cap somewhere safe where it won't get dirty or fall inside the engine bay.

2

ADD OIL

Slowly add some oil, giving it 30 seconds to a minute to drain to the bottom of the engine. Use a funnel to prevent spilling. Cut the top off a clean plastic bottle to make a homemade funnel.

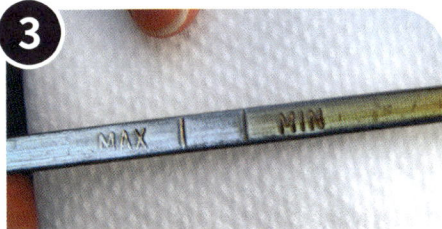

3

RECHECK LEVEL

Now you've added some oil, recheck the level on the dipstick. If you need to, add more oil until you reach the MAX mark.

4

REPLACE FILLER CAP

When you've finished topping up, screw the oil filler cap back on. Double check the dipstick is securely in place.

COOLANT

BACKGROUND KNOWLEDGE

Engines run best when they are warm, so the cooling system is designed to let the engine warm up quickly and then maintain a steady temperature. In electric vehicles, coolant manages the temperature of the battery and other parts.

A water pump moves the coolant through channels in the engine or battery where it picks up heat. The coolant then travels to the radiator where the heat is transferred to the air. It's a bit like the central heating system in a house, where the boiler creates heat.

If your car is overheating you should stop straight away. If it's not safe to stop, turn the heater to hot and the fan speed to max. This helps to draw heat away from the engine.

Generally, a car needs to be moving for the heat from the radiator to be transferred to the air. To stop the car overheating when you're sitting in traffic, a fan is fitted to the radiator that switches on if the coolant starts to get too hot.

An important things about coolant is its higher boiling point and lower freezing point compared to water. The higher boiling point (around 106°C) stops it becoming a gas which is no good at transferring heat. A lower freezing point (around -37°C) stops parts like pipes from cracking on a sub-zero day.

There seem to be many types of antifreeze, what's the difference?

The obvious difference between types of antifreeze is colour. However, the most important difference is the chemicals added to prevent corrosion of the cooling system. You'll find some types of antifreeze are long life, lasting five years instead of two for example. As a general rule, stick to what the car manufacturer recommends. However, most different types of antifreeze can be mixed without serious side effects. The most important thing is to make sure the coolant level is topped up and the concentration (50:50 mix) is correct.

WHAT TO BUY

You can buy antifreeze as either a concentrate or ready mixed with water. Ready mixed will save you time and is more convenient as you won't need a separate container to mix it in. It also saves you the bother of measuring out the right quantities, but it can work out slightly more expensive than mixing it yourself.

If you buy concentrated antifreeze make sure you have some distilled water to mix it with. Tap water should never be used as it contains impurities that cause corrosion inside the cooling system.

Distilled water is sometimes called de-ionised water. You may have some at home for use in your iron.

"A 'mayonnaise' type gunk in the coolant tank is a result of the coolant coming into contact with oil. This is usually caused by a leak inside the engine allowing them to mix and should be investigated by a garage straight away."

What's the difference between coolant and antifreeze?

Coolant is the product of mixing water and antifreeze together, usually in a 50:50 ratio. As well as lower freezing and higher boiling points, antifreeze also contains chemicals that prevent corrosion inside the engine and cooling system.

CHECK YOUR
COOLANT

On most cars the coolant tank is made from see-through plastic. You shouldn't need to remove the cap to check the level but if you do, make sure you've given the car time to cool down. (Read the warnings under topping up.) If you have trouble seeing the coolant level, shine a torch through the tank or rock it gently from side to side and you should see it swishing around. If you are losing coolant regularly, get the car checked over as soon as possible.

💡 Keep a bottle of water in the boot in case you need to make an emergency top up.

1

LOCATE COOLANT TANK

The coolant tank should be see-through so you won't need to remove the cap to check the level. If you do, make sure you've let the car cool down first.

2

FIND MIN / MAX MARKS

The MIN and MAX levels should be clearly marked on the side of the tank. Anywhere between these marks is acceptable, but if close to the minimum, it's worth topping up.

3

RADIATOR CAP

If you have an older car, the cap may be directly attached to the radiator. Remove it to check the level making sure you let the car cool down first.

4

LOOK INSIDE

With the cap off, look inside the neck of the radiator. The coolant level should be above the metal grill. (Shown by the arrow in the picture.)

TOP-UP YOUR
COOLANT

The cooling system works under high pressure and will stay pressurised for some time after you've driven the car. Always let it cool down before removing the coolant cap or boiling fluid could spray out and scald you. When unscrewing the cap, do it slowly as if you are opening a fizzy drinks bottle that's been shaken. You'll hear a similar hissing noise as the pressure releases. Using a bit of cloth will give you a good grip on the cap and help protect your hands.

If you're mixing coolant from antifreeze and distilled water, make sure you have a clean container to mix them in.

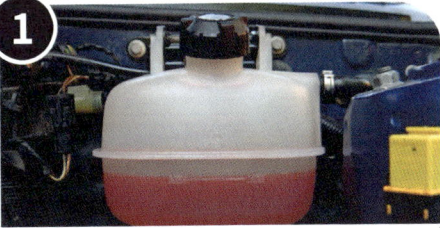

LOCATE COOLANT TANK

If you've just driven the car, make sure you let it cool down before carefully removing the coolant cap. Place the cap somewhere safe where it won't fall inside the engine bay.

TOP-UP COOLANT

Add the coolant but be careful not to overfill. Use a funnel to prevent spilling. (Cut the top off a clean plastic bottle to make a homemade funnel.)

REPLACE CAP

Once you've topped up to the MAX mark replace the cap securely.

OLDER CARS

A similar top up procedure applies for adding coolant directly to the radiator. Make sure the coolant covers the area at the top of the radiator shown by the arrow.

BRAKE FLUID

BACKGROUND KNOWLEDGE

Brake fluid transmits the force you apply on the pedal to the brake pads which are squeezed against a metal disk. The resulting friction between them generates a huge amount of heat, so brake fluid has to withstand extreme temperatures which can exceed 500°C.

With very heavy use the brakes can get so hot that the fluid boils and becomes a gas. As gas can be squashed, the force you apply to the brake pedal is no longer transferred to the brakes as efficiently. This is known as 'brake fade'. When this starts to happen you'll find yourself pushing the brake pedal further towards the floor than normal before the car starts to slow. (Sometimes descibed as the brake pedal becoming 'long'.)

Test your brakes if you've driven through deep water. Applying light pressure to the brake pedal will help dry them out.

A common time for this to occur is during extended periods of braking, such as a long descent down a steep hill. To prevent the brakes and brake fluid from overheating, use the gears to slow the car down rather than constantly having the brakes applied. If you notice brake fade, stop and allow the brakes to cool down.

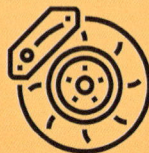

My brakes have started squealing, what's wrong?

Brake squeal can simply be a result of cold weather or excess moisture around the brakes but should only be temporary. If your brakes are squealing regularly, it's often a sign that the brake pads are worn down. Any problems with the brakes should be checked straight away, especially grinding noises which indicates something more serious is wrong.

WHAT TO BUY

The most common type of brake fluid is called DOT 4. A new bottle of DOT 4 will have a foil seal under the cap to keep it air tight. Once open, brake fluid will start to absorb moisture from the air which makes it less effective when added to the braking system. You can buy brake fluid in various size bottles but it's best to buy the smallest one possible. You'll replace a small bottle more frequently and reduce the amount of time the fluid is exposed to air.

The other types of brake fluid you'll come across are called DOT 3 and DOT 5. DOT 3 has the same chemical makeup as DOT 4 but is a lower specification. DOT 5 is completely different and should never be mixed with the other two.

For help finding the right fluid, you can visit a motorspares website. Alternatively, check your car's handbook or call a local dealership for advice on the correct fluid to use.

Why does brake fluid need changing regularly?

Brake fluid becomes less effective over time as it absorbs water. Because water boils at a lower temperature than brake fluid it often results in a 'spongy' feel from the pedal. Having the brake fluid changed at regular service intervals will make sure the brakes are operating as effectively as possible and stop water from causing corrosion inside the brake pipes.

Comma
Brake & Clutch Fluid
DOT 4
Synthetic
REMVLOEISTOF
LIQUIDE DE
FRIEN

CHECK YOUR
BRAKE FLUID

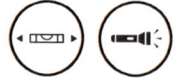

Most brake fluid reservoir bottles are made from see-through plastic, which makes it easy to check the level. Just make sure it's the brake fluid you've located and not the power steering bottle. The brake fluid reservoir is usually at the back of the engine bay, in front of the steering wheel. Avoid taking off the cap when checking the level to stop excess moisture from the air being absorbed by the brake fluid.

💡 Dirt and grease can clog up the braking system, so make sure the area around the cap is clean before you remove it.

1

FIND THE BRAKE FLUID BOTTLE
The level of the brake fluid should be visible through the bottle and is a pale yellow colour. Try to avoid removing the cap to check the level.

2

LOCATE MIN / MAX MARKS
Find the MIN and MAX marks which should be clearly marked on the side of the brake fluid reservoir.

3

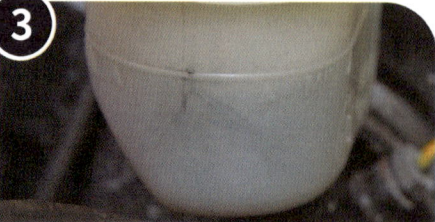

CHECK THE LEVEL
Check the level is between the minimum and maximum marks. If it's anywhere close to the minimum you'll need to top up.

4

SHAKE THE TANK
If you're having trouble seeing exactly where the level is, try shaking the bottle gently. Alternatively, shining a torch through the side may help.

TOP-UP YOUR
BRAKE FLUID

Brake fluid is very corrosive and will strip the paint off a car, so you'll want to avoid getting any on your hands. As a precaution, use a pair of rubber gloves to protect your hands and have some water ready to wash any spilt fluid off the car as quickly as possible.

The brake fluid level falls naturally over time as the brakes wear, but if you're having to top up often, the car should be checked for leaks.

1

FIND THE BRAKE FLUID BOTTLE

Wipe away any grease and dirt from around the cap.

2

REMOVE CAP

Remove the cap and place it on a clean bit of rag or kitchen roll. Make sure it's somewhere it can't drop into the engine bay. Be careful not to get any brake fluid on your hands or the car's paintwork.

3

TOP-UP BRAKE FLUID

Add the brake fluid until you reach the MAX mark.

4

REPLACE CAP

Replace the cap straight away to stop moisture in the air being absorbed by the brake fluid.

POWER STEERING FLUID

Power Assisted Steering (you might see it abbreviated as 'PAS') reduces the effort required by the driver to turn the car at low speeds. It's especially helpful for manoeuvres in tight spaces such as parallel parking or making a turn in the road.

One type of assisted steering uses a pump which is powered from the engine via a rubber belt. When you steer, hydraulic fluid is pumped at high pressure to assist the turning of the wheels. If this applies to your car, the power steering fluid will require a top up from time to time. Keep a regular eye on the level by checking it at the same time as your oil level.

If your steering seems heavier than normal but the fluid level is correct, check your tyre pressures. Under-inflated tyres are a common and simple cause of heavy steering.

If the system runs low on fluid, the steering can become heavy and start to squeal or hiss. If left too long it could break down completely which is not only costly but can also be dangerous as the car may become very difficult to steer and control.

This type of hydraulic power steering has become less common, with most cars now using an electric motor to assist with the steering. See box ▶

My car has power steering, why can't I find the fluid reservoir?

To improve fuel efficiency, Electric Power Steering (often called EPS) has become the most common. Your steering inputs are assisted by a motor. In a purely electric system there is no fluid to check.

It's worth mentioning that some electric systems, known as 'electro-hydraulic', will use power steering fluid.

WHAT TO BUY

Most hydraulic power steering systems will use Automatic Transmission Fluid ('ATF' for short). However, some manufacturers recommend specific types of fluid that contain special additives to protect the rubber seals in the system. The right fluid will depend on the type of power steering you have and the make of car. For help finding the right fluid, you can visit a motorspares website. Alternatively, check your car's handbook or call a local dealership for advice on the correct fluid to use.

> **It's normal to hear the steering system 'growl' a little when full lock is applied. At any other point in between it means there is a problem.**

Why does my steering feel light in town but heavier on the motorway?

It's likely your car is fitted with 'speed sensitive steering' which varies the amount of assistance provided.

At lower speeds, greater assistance is provided which makes turning the wheel easier and helps with parking. At higher speeds, less assistance is required to change the direction of the car.

CHECK YOUR
POWER STEERING FLUID

The power steering reservoir is usually a see-through bottle and the sides are marked with MIN and MAX. On other cars without these markings, a small dipstick is attached to the underside of the reservoir cap. This dipstick will either have two marks for MIN & MAX (like the oil dipstick) or be marked with 'H' and 'C' for Hot and Cold. If you've just driven the car, the fluid level should be at the 'H'. If the car is cold the level should be at the 'C' mark.

The level of power steering fluid changes with temperature. It's best to check it when the car is fully warmed up.

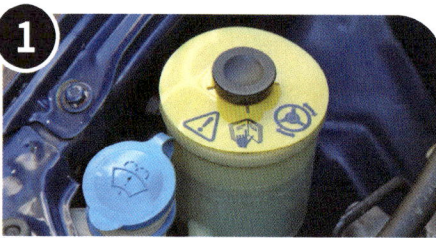

LOCATE FLUID BOTTLE

On some cars the level of the power steering fluid can be checked by looking through the bottle. If your car is like this, look at where the level lies between the MIN and MAX marks.

DIPSTICK TYPE CHECK

If your car uses a dipstick, remove the cap, wiping away any dirt and grease from around it first. Familiarise yourself with the marks, wipe the stick clean and screw the cap back on.

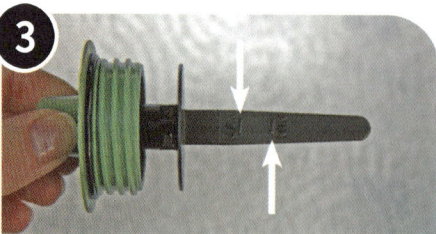

CHECK THE LEVEL

Remove the cap, this time checking the level. If the car has just been run the level should be at 'H' for Hot or 'MAX'. If the car hasn't been driven recently, the level should be at 'C' for Cold.

REPLACE CAP

When you've finished, replace the cap securely.

TOP-UP YOUR
POWER STEERING FLUID

Wipe any dirt and grease away from around the power steering cap to stop it getting into the fluid reservoir and blocking up the system. Make sure you top up to the correct level depending if the car is hot or cold.

If you're topping up often, have the car checked for leaks. A leaky hose is cheaper to fix than letting the steering pump fail.

1

LOCATE FLUID BOTTLE
Wipe away any grease and dirt from around the cap.

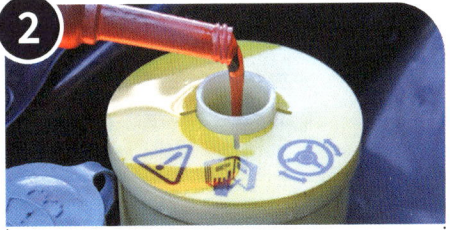

2

TOP-UP
Locate the level marks on the side and top up the power steering fluid until you reach the max.

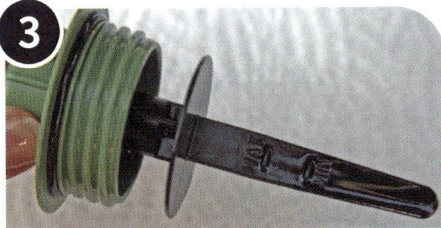

3

TOP-UP — DIPSTICK TYPE
If your car has a dipstick to show the level, top up with a small amount and then re-check the level. If the car is hot top up to the 'H' or 'MAX' mark and 'C' if the car is cold.

4

REPLACE CAP
Replace the cap securely when you've finished.

SCREEN WASH

BACKGROUND KNOWLEDGE

The four main parts of a windscreen washer system are; a large container that holds the washer fluid, a pump, jets which direct the washer fluid at the windscreen and lengths of hose that connect it all together. Despite its relative simplicity, the washer system is an important safety feature of the car and must be in good working order for your car to pass its MOT.

Your car's head lamps get just as grimy as the windscreen. Give them a wipe when topping up with washer fluid and more often during the winter.

WHAT TO BUY

Screen wash comes either ready mixed or as a concentrate. Ready mixed comes in different strengths designed for summer or winter, with winter mixes being stronger to cut through the heavy road grime. You can also get washer fluid that includes de-icer and even some with added scents. (If you want the outside of your car to smell like apples or berries!)

Can I just fill the washer bottle with tap water?

You can but there's a chance the whole system could freeze up in winter. Screen wash contains a mild antifreeze to help prevent this. Pure tap water also won't be as good at cutting through road grime either. Think of it like cleaning the dishes without washing up liquid.

TOP-UP YOUR
SCREEN WASH

Usually only the neck of the washer fluid bottle is visible, with the bulk of it tucked out of sight. Some cars have a second washer bottle in the boot for the rear wash/wipe, so you might need to top this up too. If you're using ready mixed screen wash buy a stronger formula for winter. If you're mixing it yourself, 1:5 screen wash to water is about right for summer and 1:2 for winter, depending on how grimy the roads are and how cold it is.

> Don't use washing up liquid to make a screen wash mix. The salt and detergents will damage the paintwork.

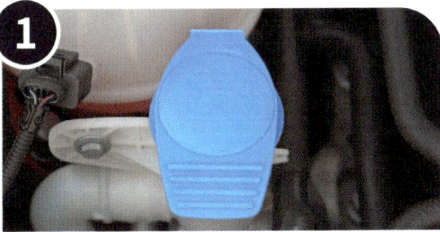

1

LOCATE WASHER FLUID CAP
Locate the washer bottle cap. Remember, there could be a second bottle in the boot if your car is fitted with a rear wiper.

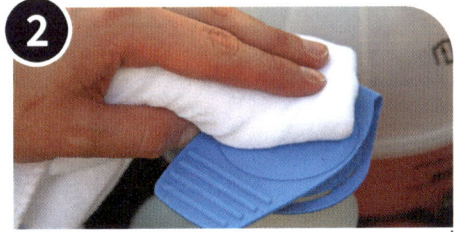

2

WIPE AWAY DIRT
Wipe away dirt from the cap to stop it causing a blockage. Washer bottles sometimes have a filter in the neck that stops the dirt getting in. You may need to clean this out from time to time.

3

USE A FUNNEL
Use a funnel to add the washer fluid as the big containers are heavy and awkward to pour.

4

FINISH WHEN FOAMING
The washer bottle will be full enough when it starts to foam up at the cap.

AIR CONDITIONING

BACKGROUND KNOWLEDGE

If your car is fitted with air conditioning, the last thing you'll want is it packing up on one of those rare hot summer days! Air conditioning maintenance is easily overlooked as it doesn't tend to affect the roadworthiness of the car. However, neglecting it can lead to expensive problems further down the line.

Basic upkeep is easy and will help ensure it's working when you need it. One of the simplest ways you can keep your air conditioning in good order is to use it all year round. Try using it at least once every two weeks.

In winter, use your air conditioning to demist the windscreen. It's an easy way to make sure you use it all year round and is very good at clearing the screen.

What happens if I don't use the air conditioning very often?

When used infrequently, moisture can start to build up in the pipes and vents which breeds fungus, bacteria and mould. This can make the car smell like old socks or worse, gives you a sore throat and headache. You can prevent and cure this yourself by using an air conditioning cleaner. Other maintenance will need to be done by a professional, for instance, changing the air filters which get blocked with dust and pollen.

The refrigerant gas that the system runs on will need refilling every two to three years as it escapes gradually over time and leaves you with air-conditioning that no longer blows cold. A lack of use increases the rate at which the gas escapes as the rubber joints in the system dry out and no longer form a good seal.

WHAT TO BUY

Air conditioning cleaner is a cheap and effective way to clean the system yourself. You can either buy it as an aerosol can which is sprayed directly into the air vents, or the type that is left to discharge inside the car with the air conditioning running. You'll find it on sale in most motor spares stores.

AIR CONDITIONING PROBLEM SOLVER

LEAK? If you've been driving the car with the air conditioning running, you may find small puddles on the ground under the car after it's been parked. This will usually be where a drain tube is fitted to the system that allows condensation to escape.

However, if you notice it regularly, check your coolant level to make sure you don't have a leak, especially if you haven't been using the air conditioning.

MISTING? If your windscreen mists up excessively or the carpets seem damp it could mean the condensation drain pipe is blocked. If you have this problem it's an easy thing to have fixed. (And definitely worth it to stop any bacteria and mould growing.)

FUNNY NOISES? Strange noises that start when you run the air conditioning should get immediate attention. The system pump called the 'compressor' could be the cause and is often a sign of it failing. It might not be cheap to fix but will be significantly cheaper than letting the entire system breakdown.

FUSES

BACKGROUND KNOWLEDGE

A fuse contains a thin piece of wire designed to melt if the electric current passing through it is too high. If the current exceeds the fuse rating, it will blow to protect the circuit and equipment from being overloaded. Every electrical circuit in the car is protected by a fuse; your radio, the heated rear window, even the horn.

Modern cars have 'blade fuses' which come in three common sizes. The largest, called 'maxi', are used in high power circuits and are often found in a secondary fuse box under the bonnet (see page 11). The fuse box in the passenger compartment could contain either 'Mini' or 'ATO' fuses or a mixture of the two. These are used in the majority of a car's electric systems.

All blade fuses are made from coloured plastic which indicates their rating. It will also be marked in writing either on the top or on one of the metal legs.

Where can I find the fusebox?

A lot of cars have two fuse boxes; one under the bonnet and one inside the car. The fuse box under the bonnet tends to be for higher capacity circuits, such as the one used to start the car. The other fuse box will be located inside the car. The most common places to find it are behind the glovebox, by the driver's legs under the steering column or behind a panel at the end of the dashboard (only accessible when the door is open).

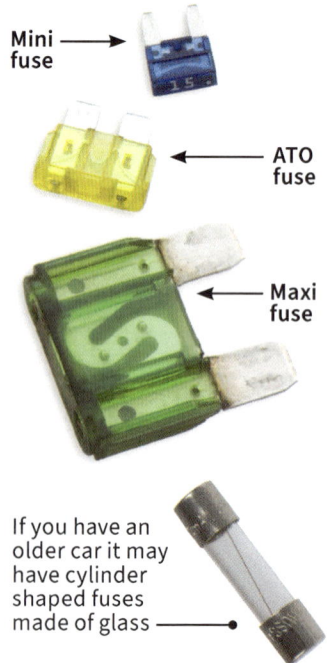

Mini → fuse

ATO fuse

Maxi fuse

If you have an older car it may have cylinder shaped fuses made of glass

A fuse box will usually contain a diagram (often on the fusebox lid) with symbols or writing that show the circuit a fuse covers and its rating. If you can't work out what some of the symbols mean, the handbook should contain the same diagram with a description of each symbol.

HEATER MOTOR	15A	20A	HAZARD LAMPS
WASH WIPE	15A	10A	INTERIOR LIGHTS
MIRRORS	10A		
RADIO	10A	5A	REVERSE SENSORS
USB	5A	10A	CENTRAL LOCKING
HEATED WINDOW	10A		
HEAD LAMP	10A	20A	REAR FOG
TURN SIGNAL	10A	20A	FRONT FOGS
CLOCK	5A	30A	PAS

▲ Example of what you might find on the lid of your fusebox

Blade fuses can be checked visually to see if they have blown. In a blown fuse the metal in the centre that connects the two flat blades will have melted.

▲ Blown fuse

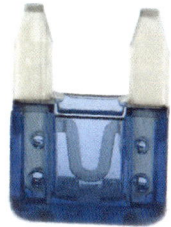
▲ Good fuse

Most fuse boxes will have a set of plastic tweezers to help you pull out the fuse. ▼

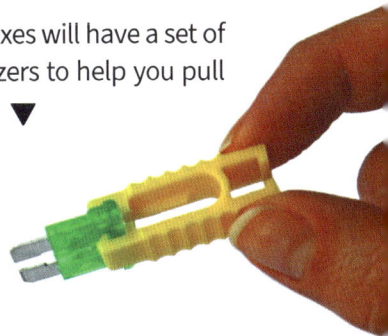

If a fuse keeps blowing, first check the rating of the fuse is correct. It could simply be that the fuse has been incorrectly replaced with one of a lower rating i.e 10 amp instead of 15 amp. If this doesn't correct the fault get the car checked out professionally.

CHANGE A
FUSE

If a fuse has blown on an important circuit, such as the indicators, and you have no replacement, take out the blown fuse and replace it with one from a non-essential circuit, such as the interior lights or cigarette lighter. Never put in a higher rated fuse than the one you are removing or is stated in the handbook. It could allow too much current to flow and damage the equipment it's designed to protect. (It could even cause an electrical fire.)

The fuse box usually contains a few spare fuses but it's worth getting a set of mixed fuses to keep in the glovebox.

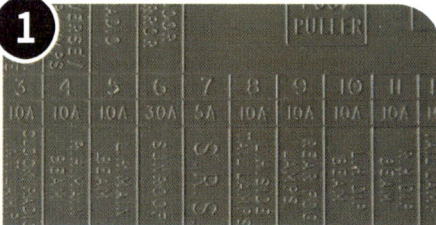

FIND THE RIGHT FUSE

Use the car handbook or the lid of the fuse box to help identify which fuse you need to remove.

REMOVE FUSE

In the fuse box you should find a small set of plastic tweezers that make removing a fuse much easier. Simply slip them over the end of the fuse and pull it out.

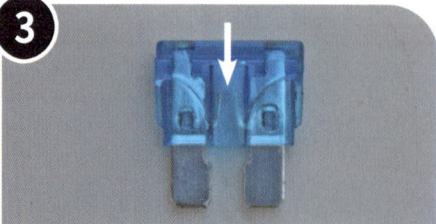

CHECK FUSE

If the fuse has blown, the thin metal wire that connects the two flat blades will be broken.

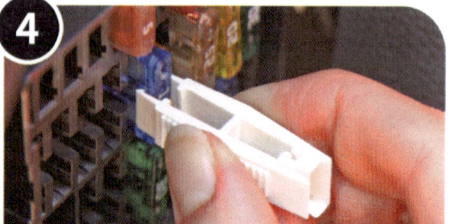

REPLACE FUSE

Use the fuse tweezers to insert the new fuse. Make sure the fuse you are putting in is the same rating as the one you took out.

BULBS

BACKGROUND KNOWLEDGE

Changing a bulb isn't usually a difficult job but it can be made very tricky by limited access and what might need to be removed to get to it. On quite a few cars the battery has to be taken out before you can get to a headlight bulb. In more extreme cases the bumper has to be removed to get to a front fog light. More and more modern cars are also fitted with LED light units. This usually means bulbs can't be replaced and instead, the whole unit needs to be replaced.

However, some can be very simple, so changing a bulb isn't something you should be afraid of having a go at. Just bear in mind that how easy it is varies a great deal from one car to the next. If you find you can't do it or don't fancy trying in the first place, a dealer or motor spares store will be able to do the job.

WHAT TO BUY

A bulb kit is a very handy thing to keep in your car and a legal requirement in some European countries. Most bulb kits will contain a spare for all the major bulbs such as the headlights, sidelights, brakes lights and indicators. You'll often get some spare fuses in the kit as well. You can pick up a bulb kit either from a main dealer or a motor spares store.

Why are my indicators flashing faster than usual?

This is the tell-tale sign that one of the indicator bulbs has blown. Find out which one by putting the hazards on and taking a walk around the car.

CHANGING
BULBS

All light fittings are different; the guides in this section will show you the common principles for changing a few different types of bulb. On your car some might be easy and others not. Remember too, it may not be possible at all if your car has LED units. Before you attempt anything, check the car's handbook, it will usually say if the bulb is a job only a garage can do.

> Be careful not to touch the glass part of the bulb. The oils left by your skin can cause the bulb to shatter when it heats up.

HEADLIGHT ▼

REMOVE PLASTIC CAP

Remove the cover, giving you access to the plug at the back of the bulb. In some cases you'll find a rubber cover instead of the cap. The plug may need to be removed first, before the rubber.

UNPLUG BULB

A plastic plug is pushed onto the back of the bulb. You need to remove this. They can be quite tight on the bulb, so gently wiggle from side to side if you're having trouble getting it off.

RELEASE BULB

To release the bulb, unhook the wires from the metal notches. Push the clip down and to one side of them. On your car you may find there is only one clip holding the bulb.

WITHDRAW BULB

You should now be able to remove the bulb from the headlamp. Note the way the notches on the bulb match the grooves on the headlamp casing.

1 REMOVE COVER / TRIM

You'll need to gain access to the back of the light unit from inside the boot. It may simply be a case of removing a plastic cover, but sometimes parts of the boot trim will need to be removed.

2 REMOVE BULB HOLDER

To remove the bulb holder, there is usually a set of clips that you squeeze. Whilst squeezing these clips, withdraw the bulb holder.

3 CHECK / REMOVE BULBS

Blown bulbs will have a broken wire inside or the glass may appear black. To remove, push down and twist gently. The bulb should release and spring gently up from the holder.

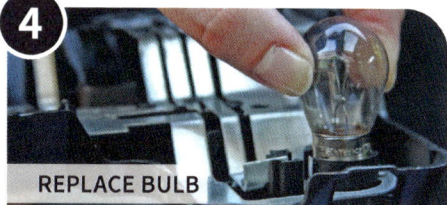

4 REPLACE BULB

To replace, line up the notches on the bulb with the ones on the casing. Push the bulb in and then twist to lock it into place. Wipe the bulb clean if your fingers have touched the glass.

— **BRAKE LIGHT ▲** ——————— **SIDE INDICATOR ▼** —

1 RELEASE INDICATOR

Side indicators may fit in a hole in the wing. A plastic spring often holds it in place. (See the arrow picture 3.) Push on the lens to squeeze the spring and release the indicator.

2 REMOVE LENS

As you squeeze the plastic spring, use your other hand to pull the indicator lens towards you. You shouldn't need a lot of force to release it. Try sliding it in a different direction instead of forcing it.

3 SEPARATE BULB HOLDER

Twist the back part of the indicator lamp and pull it towards you. This separates the indicator lens. Keep hold of the back part with the wires, as it can disappear back into the wing.

4 CHANGE BULB

Remove the bulb, gently pulling it from the holder. Wipe away finger marks on the glass when refitting. Line up the notches on the holder with the grooves in the lens and twist back together.

BATTERY CARE

BACKGROUND KNOWLEDGE

This section refers to the 12-volt battery system in a car. Even if your car is a hybrid or electric it will normally have a 12 volt system. This runs things like the radio and the wipers. Unless you're very lucky, you'll probably get stuck with a flat battery at least once. The most common cause is forgetting to switch headlights off or using the heater or a portable hoover when the car isn't running.

A flat battery is the most common cause of breakdowns in winter, as cold weather slows down the chemical reactions inside it. A cold snap can easily flatten a battery without warning, with the power becoming too low to start the car.

If your engine is taking longer to start than usual, especially in winter, get it checked before it's too late. A higher load is put on a battery in winter, when you run the heater, headlights, wipers and rear window heaters more often. Finally, a lack of fluid in the battery (called electrolyte) can cause the battery to become faulty. This is an easy thing to keep an eye on and top up if required.

If you buy a new battery, put the receipt straight in the glovebox. If there's ever a problem within the battery warranty period, you'll have it easily to hand.

How does a car battery recharge?

The battery is charged by the alternator which is turned by a belt powered from the engine. This means it only recharges the battery when the engine is running.

Starting the car takes a lot of power from the battery which needs to be replaced. On a short journey the alternator doesn't have time to fully recharge it. As a result, the battery in a car used mainly for short trips will have a shorter lifespan.

WHAT TO BUY

Distilled water is used to top up the battery fluid. It's easy to do and helps prolong the lifespan of the battery. If the level gets low the metal plates inside the battery can buckle, reducing the output power from the battery. You should never use tap water to top up the fluid in a battery.

PRECAUTIONS!

1. The gas given off by a car battery is explosive. More gas is given off when charging or jump-starting, so don't smoke or allow any naked flames nearby.

2. If the battery casing is cracked it should be replaced to stop the corrosive fluids leaking into the engine bay.

3. If your radio has a security code, you'll have to enter it if the battery has been disconnected. The code should be in the same wallet as the car manual, often on a separate bit of paper about the size of a credit card.

4. Be careful not to let metal objects like the blade of a screwdriver or a wrist watch touch the battery terminals. The resulting short circuit could damage the electrics and the sparks could ignite the gas given off by the battery, causing an explosion.

5. Some batteries are 'maintenance free' and can't be topped up with distilled water. If the indicator on the top of the battery is showing flat, it shouldn't be charged as the level of electrolyte may be too low and there is an increased risk of explosion. (See over the page.)

CHECK YOUR
BATTERY FLUID

In most cars the 12-volt battery is under the bonnet, however in some cars the battery is in the boot. You may need to empty the boot and pull up the mat to find it. A twenty pence coin is often the easiest way to unscrew the plastic caps on the battery. If your battery is 'maintenance free', a small window on the top shows you its status. (See photo.) The fluid in a maintenance free battery can't be checked or topped up.

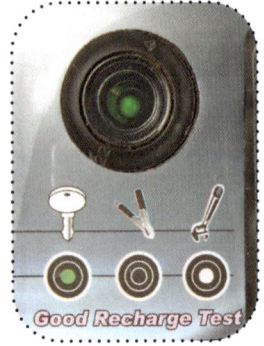

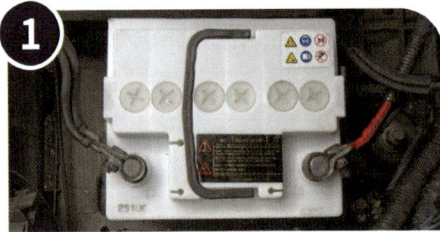

Good Recharge Test

1 LOCATE BATTERY
In most cars the battery will be under the bonnet of the car, however in some cars the battery is in the boot.

2 REMOVE CAPS
On the top of the battery there will usually be six round circles with a 'screw head' like cross on them. Each of these can be removed individually by unscrewing them.

3 CHECK FLUID LEVEL
The fluid level should cover the metal plates. If they are not fully covered, add some distilled water. (You might need a torch to see inside but don't use a lighter or any naked flame.)

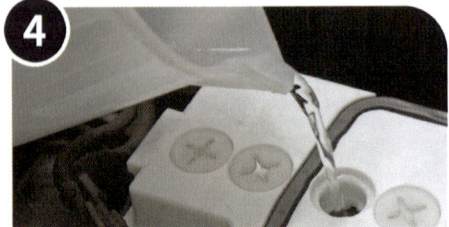

4 TOP-UP IF NEEDED
Top up with distilled water if needed. Check each hole and then make sure all the plastic screws are back in place securely.

JUMP STARTING

BACKGROUND KNOWLEDGE

Compared to other parts of the car, the lifetime of a 12-volt battery is relatively short. Usually around five years depending on the types of journey you make, how often you use the car and even factors like the weather. The following section is based on jump starting a traditionally powered car (i.e. an internal combusion engine that uses petrol or diesel.)

Jump starting a hybrid or electric car is possible in some cases, but there are some important precautions to take and specific procedures to follow, as these vehicles have unique electrical systems compared to traditional internal combustion engine vehicles. For hybrid cars, the 12-volt battery can often be jump-started using a similar process to a conventional vehicle, but always consult your owner's manual for specific instructions.

For a fully electric vehicle (EV), you should never attempt to jump-start the high-voltage battery (the one that powers the motor), as this can be extremely dangerous and may damage the battery or electrical components. However, some EVs have a separate 12-volt battery that powers the vehicle's accessories and control systems. In this case, you may be able to jump-start the 12-volt battery using the recommended procedure in the owner's manual.

Never attempt to work on the high-voltage system of an electric car.

Electric vehicles use high-voltage battery packs and electrical components, which can carry voltages ranging from 200V to over 800V, depending on the vehicle. Direct or indirect contact with these high-voltage components can lead to risk or death or serious injury, including electrocution and burns.

To minimize the risks associated with working on an electric vehicle's high-voltage system, only qualified personnel with specialist training and equipment should perform maintenance or repairs on these systems.

Keep in mind that if the 12-volt battery in your hybrid or electric vehicle is dead, there may be an underlying issue that needs to be addressed by a mechanic.

CONTINUED:
JUMP STARTING

BACKGROUND KNOWLEDGE

To understand how you can help prolong the life of the battery and avoid having to jump start your car, take a look at these common causes of a flat 12-volt battery.

SHORT JOURNEYS: Starting the car takes a lot of power from the battery and on a short journey there may not be enough time to recharge and replace this power. Frequent short trips may eventually leave the battery without enough power to start the car.

LACK OF USE: Even when parked, systems like the alarm and immobiliser will draw a small amount of power and over time can run the battery down.

WRONG BATTERY: If the battery has been replaced with one that's less powerful than specified by the manufacturer it can go flat very quickly.

COLD WEATHER: Winter is the busiest time of year for breakdown services and the biggest cause of call outs is flat batteries. Cold weather slows down the chemical reactions in the battery, reducing its power. Winter is also when you're likely to be putting it under the greatest strain, running electrical systems such as the heater, the lights and windscreen wipers.

HEADLIGHTS LEFT ON: The headlights draw a large amount of power and will flatten the battery very quickly if the car isn't running. Always leave the lights switched off until you have started the car.

FAULTY CHARGING SYSTEM: The main part of the charging system is the alternator. It looks like a large motor and is driven by a belt attached to the engine. If the alternator is faulty, the battery isn't charged properly and will eventually go flat. If your battery does fail unexpectedly, ask for the alternator to be checked when the battery is replaced or you could soon end up with another flat battery.

WHAT TO BUY

To jump start a car from another you'll need a set of jump leads. Jump leads are simply one red and one black cable with clips at either end to grip the battery terminals. The difference between cheap and expensive jump leads is usually the power they can handle. A large battery in a car with a big engine will put out a lot of power and could overheat and melt a thin set of jump leads. Invest in the best set you can afford even if you only have a small car, as you might need to jump start from a larger vehicle.

Check your handbook to make sure it's safe to jump start your car. Some cars have sensitive electrical systems that may be damaged by jump starting.

A jump start pack is essentially a portable car battery and comes with leads that you connect straight to the battery. Although more expensive than jump leads, the advantage is that you won't need to rely on the power source of another car. Jump packs often have a feature that prevents damage to the electrics if you accidentally connect the leads the wrong way round. Some also come with extras such as a light, a built in tyre inflator or even a household plug socket that can run low powered electrical items such as a laptop.

HOW TO
JUMP START

If you're jump-starting from another vehicle, make sure the batteries are the same voltage. Most cars are 12v, motorbikes 6v and lorries 24v. Don't attempt to jump start a battery that looks damaged and keep metal objects away from the top of the battery to avoid causing a spark that might trigger an explosion. Once you've got the car going, avoid using non-essential electrical systems such as the radio.

Make sure the two cars are not touching and the jump leads are not near any moving parts in the engine bay.

JUMP PACK ▼

1

CONNECT LEAD TO PACK

If required, connect the jump leads to the power pack. Make sure the unit is charged and has enough power to jump start the car.

2

CONNECT LEADS TO BATTERY

Connect the positive (red) lead to the positive terminal of the battery. Connect the negative (black) lead to the negative terminal.

3

PRECAUTIONS

Make sure the leads are out of the way of any moving parts and are securely connected. Check the jump pack is secure and won't move when the engine starts.

4

START THE CAR

Start the car. Remove the leads in reverse order (negative then positive). Be careful not to touch them on the body of the car.

JUMP START: CAR TO CAR ▼

1

LINE UP CARS

Check where the batteries are located on both cars, then line them up so the leads reach between the two batteries. Make sure the cars are not touching each other.

2

SWITCH OFF

Switch off both cars, make sure they are not in gear and handbrakes are on. (Automatics should be placed in PARK.) Turn off any electric systems like the heater or headlights on both cars.

3

CONNECT POSITIVES

Connect the red lead to the positive terminal of the good battery. Connect the other end to the positive on the flat battery. Be careful not to touch any body work.

4

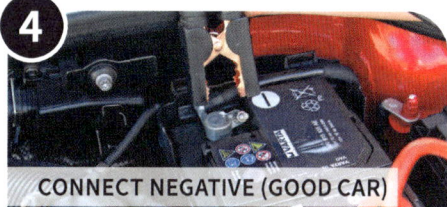

CONNECT NEGATIVE (GOOD CAR)

Take the black lead and connect it to the negative on the good battery.

5

CONNECT NEGATIVE (FLAT CAR)

Take the other end of the black lead and connect to a metal bracket on the engine as far from the flat battery as possible. Check both leads are away from any moving parts and the clamps are secure.

6

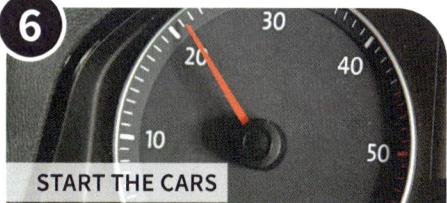

START THE CARS

Start the good car and rev to around 2000 rpm. After a couple of minutes, try starting the flat car. If the flat car doesn't start within 10 seconds then stop trying and call for breakdown assistance.

7

LEAVE CARS CONNECTED

Once the flat car has been started, keep both cars connected and running for up to 10 minutes. Keep an eye on the jump leads for overheating. Switch off immediately if they get too hot.

8

SWITCH OFF

Switch both cars off and disconnect the leads in the following order. **1.** Negative flat car. **2.** Negative good car. **3.** Positive flat car. **4.** Positive good car. Be careful not to let the leads touch.

TYRES

....

BACKGROUND KNOWLEDGE

Tyres are the most important safety feature on your car, carrying its weight and dealing with the forces of accelerating, braking and cornering. The diagram below illustrates the information that's moulded onto the side of every tyre. You'll need this when getting a quote for new tyres.

REPLACING TYRES: Tyres should always be replaced in pairs i.e. a front set or a rear set to avoid any handling or balance problems under braking.

CHOOSING TYRES: Always choose the best tyres you can afford. Budget tyres can provide similar grip to premium tyres in the dry, but there is often a much bigger difference in their wet weather performance. It's especially important to buy tyres that perform well in the wet as it rains an average of 155 days a year in the UK!

TYRE SIZE: It's a legal requirement that both front tyres are the same size and both rear tyres are the same size. However, the front set can be a different size from the rear set. A wheel will only accept certain tyre sizes and it's best to stick with the manufacturer's recommendation. If you do change the size of the wheels, the accuracy of your speedo will be affected (larger wheels will underestimate your speed). Lower profile tyres tend to make the ride more bumpy and increase noise inside the car.

SPEED RATING AND LOAD INDEX

The load index and speed rating of a tyre is shown by a letter and a number, for instance 79T. The number refers to the maximum load the tyre can carry and the letter refers to the maximum speed at which it can carry that load.

Example (as circled on charts below): 79T = 437kg at 118 miles per hour

From the speed rating table you can see all tyres are rated in excess of the UK speed limit. However, the speed rating gives an indication of the tyres all round performance and its ability to cope with braking, cornering and accelerating.

Don't be tempted to go for a lower speed rating than recommended by the car's manufacturer. You could end up compromising the car's handling ability and your safety.

The Load Index table doesn't list all possible values but covers most normal road cars. Values shown are per tyre.

SPEED RATING

SPEED SYMBOL	MPH	KPH	SPEED SYMBOL	MPH	KPH
M	81	130	H	130	210
P	93	150	V	150	240
Q	99	160	W	169	270
R	106	170	Y	187	300
S	112	180	ZR	150+	240+
T	118	190			

LOAD INDEX

LOAD INDEX	LOAD kg	LOAD INDEX	LOAD kg	LOAD INDEX	LOAD kg
65	290	77	412	89	580
66	300	78	425	90	600
67	307	79	437	91	615
68	315	80	450	92	630
69	325	81	462	93	650
70	335	82	475	94	670
71	345	83	487	95	690
72	355	84	500	96	710
73	365	85	515	97	730
74	375	86	530	98	750
75	387	87	545	99	775
76	400	88	560	100	800

CONTINUED:
TYRES

BACKGROUND KNOWLEDGE

BALANCE: Tyres are never completely evenly weighted and tend to have heavy spots. When the tyres are rotating, these heavy spots can cause vibration through the steering wheel, making the car uncomfortable to drive and causing unnecessary wear to the tyres, suspension and steering. A wheel can be balanced by using a machine to find the heavy spot and a weight added to counteract it. Wheels should always be balanced when the tyres are replaced, but will also need balancing during their lifetime as the tyres wear.

As a guide you should get your wheels balanced every 10,000 miles.

TRACKING: Tracking is the direction the wheels face in relation to each other and should run parallel. Poor tracking can cause a car to pull to one side and is a common cause of premature tyre wear, often visible as one side of the tread being more worn than the other. Driving over pot holes or hitting a wheel on the kerb can cause the tracking to become misaligned. To prolong the life of your tyres, suspension and steering, have your tracking checked every 10,000 miles.

◀ Tracking OK

Tracking Out ▶

Looking from above at a car with incorrect tracking, one or both front wheels could point either outwards or inwards.

DIRECTIONAL TYRES: High performance tyres sometimes have tread patterns which are only designed to rotate in one direction. This generally improves handling and grip but when fitted the wrong way round, aren't able to clear water effectively and may cause the car to become unstable. If you get a puncture and the spare tyre is directional, you may have no choice but to put it on the wrong side of the car. If you find yourself in this situation, drive carefully and at a reduced speed.

"A directional tyre will have an arrow clearly marked on the sidewall indicating the direction it should rotate."

REPAIRS: In some cases a punctured tyre can be repaired rather than replaced but only if the puncture is within the tread area and if it hasn't been driven too far when flat. Damage to the side wall creates a serious weakness in the tyre and should always be replaced.

SPACE SAVERS: Many modern cars are now provided with 'space saver' spare wheels to save weight and boot space and are thinner than the normal wheels of the car. A space saver should only be used for a limited distance, usually around 50 miles and at a maximum speed of 50mph.

RUNS FLATS: A run flat tyre is designed to let you carry on driving with a puncture without the need to change the wheel. As with space savers, run flat tyres should only be used for a limited distance and at a reduced speed.

TYRES: TREAD DEPTH

BACKGROUND KNOWLEDGE

The grooves in a tyre help channel water away and are vital for wet weather performance, affecting the car's ability to corner and brake safely. The legal minimum tread depth in the UK is 1.6mm across three quarters of the tyre's width. It's worth noting that the grip available with this little tread left is seriously reduced. A tyre with 1.6mm can take nearly 50% further to stop a car in the wet compared to a new tyre with 8mm of tread depth.

Driving with tyres below the 1.6mm limit is not only an MOT failure but also illegal. It will cost you a fine and 3 points on your licence per illegal tyre.

WHAT TO BUY

TREAD DEPTH GAUGE

A depth measuring gauge is easy to use and will only cost a few pounds. It's small enough to keep in the glovebox and will give an accurate measure of the tread depth of your tyres.

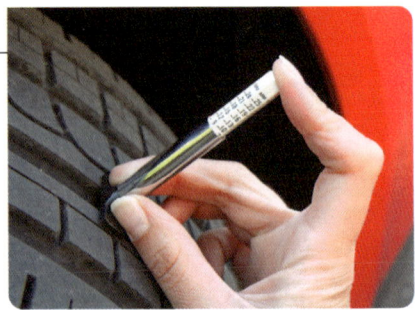

When should I think about getting new tyres?

Although the legal limit is 1.6mm, given the UK gets its fair share of rain, the safest option is to change the tyres when the depth gets down to 3mm.

CHECK YOUR
TYRE TREAD

A quick visual check of tread depth can be made by looking at the wear indicators which you'll find in the grooves of the tread pattern. This will give you a guide as to how close a tyre is to the legal limit. A tyre should be changed before the tread reaches the level of the depth indicator but ideally at 3mm.

Make sure you check all the tyres as wear rates vary, especially between the front and rear.

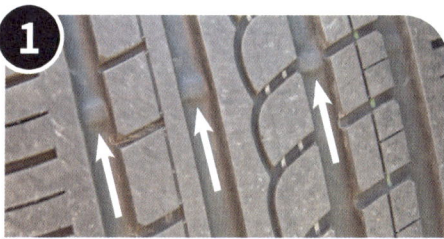

1

QUICK DEPTH CHECK

A quick visual check of tyre depth can be made by looking at the wear indicators. When the tread of the tyre is worn to the level of the indicator, it needs replacing immediately.

2

USING A DEPTH GAUGE

With a depth gauge you can get a more accurate measure of the tread. Line up the gauge over the tread and push the centre into the groove between the tread.

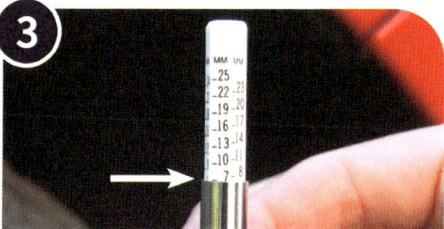

3

READ OFF DEPTH

Read the level from the gauge. In this case the tread depth is 7mm.

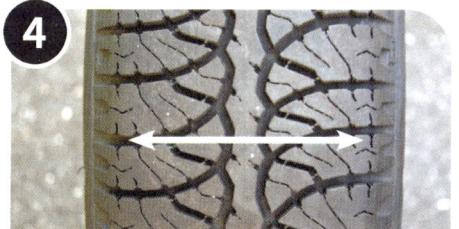

4

DEPTH ACROSS TYRE

The tread depth should be above the legal minimum of 1.6mm across three quarters of the tyre. For safety, it's wise to replace the tyres when the tread level reaches 3mm.

TYRE PRESSURES

BACKGROUND KNOWLEDGE

Tyre pressures affect grip, braking and the life of the tyre. Under-inflated tyres also make the engine work harder and use more fuel as a result. Over inflated tyres make the ride bumpy and reduce grip as less of the tyre is in contact with the road. Aim to check your tyre pressures every six to eight weeks and especially before long journeys or if you're going to carry a heavy load.

WHAT TO BUY

A pressure gauge is an easy way to check your tyres at home and comes in digital or analogue forms. (See next page.) A tyre inflator will have a pressure gauge built in and is more useful as you'll be able to top up without having to drive to a petrol station. These are mostly powered from the 12 volt cigarette lighter but can be mains powered too. Manual foot pumps are also available if you'd prefer the exercise!

Most cars have the tyre pressures printed on a sticker inside the petrol cap or on the door frame. (It will also be in the car's handbook.) This will give you the correct pressures for normal driving, higher speeds or heavy loads. Pressures are given in units of PSI or BAR.

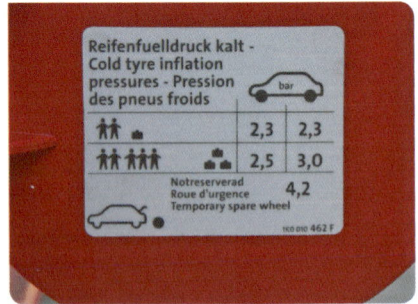

Reifenfuelldruck kalt - Cold tyre inflation pressures - Pression des pneus froids	bar	
🚶 🧳	2,3	2,3
🚶🚶 🚶🚶🚶 🧳🧳	2,5	3,0
Notreserverad Roue d'urgence Temporary spare wheel	4,2	

1K0 010 462 F

Why does one of my tyres keep going flat?

A slow loss in pressure can be caused by a faulty valve (the part where you add air to the tyre). You can check this by removing the cap and covering the valve with a little bit of washing up liquid mixed with water. If air bubbles through the liquid, the valve is leaking. Alternatively, an object like a nail may have pierced the tyre causing a 'slow puncture'.

CHECK YOUR
TYRE PRESSURES

Pressures should be checked when the tyre is cold. When the tyre gets warm the pressure increases and just a short trip to the petrol station is enough to have an effect. Don't inflate the tyre to the pressure marked on the side of it. This is the maximum inflation and not the recommended pressure. Remember that pressures for front and rear tyres are rarely the same.

💡 Don't forget to check the spare tyre. It may look inflated but can go flat when the car's weight is loaded on to it.

REMOVE DUST CAP

Remove the dust cap that covers the tyre valve. Keep it somewhere safe as they're very easy to lose on dark tarmac.

PUSH ON GAUGE

Push the nozzle of the pressure gauge securely onto the valve cap so no air can be heard escaping.

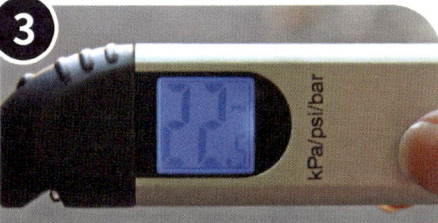

READ PRESSURE

Read off the tyre pressure in BAR or PSI and compare it to the recommended level.

REPLACE DUST CAP

If the tyre pressure is correct, replace the dust cap securely.

INFLATE YOUR
TYRES

Some inflation machines on garage forecourts are automatic. Simply input the pressure you want, put the nozzle on the valve and the rest is done for you. When the correct pressure is reached the machine will beep and you can remove the nozzle. Don't forget to top up your spare, if you have one!

Keep the valve caps in a safe place when inflating the tyres and always replace them if they go missing.

1

REMOVE DUST CAP

Remove the dust cap that covers the tyre valve. Keep it somewhere safe as they're very easy to lose on dark tarmac.

2

PUSH INFLATOR ONTO VALVE

Push the nozzle of the inflator onto the valve securely so no air can be heard escaping.

3

TOP UP TO PRESSURE

Top up to the required pressure and remove the nozzle. Don't be too slow when you remove the inflation nozzle from the valve or air will escape from the tyre.

4

OVER-INFLATION

If you over inflate the tyre, release some of the air by having the inflation nozzle half on / half off the valve so air can be heard escaping. Replace the valve caps when you've finished.

TYRE WEAR

BACKGROUND KNOWLEDGE

Uneven tyre wear will occur over time as a car gets subjected to pot-holes and speed bumps. It's also made worse by banging into kerbs when parking. A common symptom is steering wheel wobble which you may only get when travelling at higher speeds. If you notice this or spot uneven wear, have the tracking checked and the wheels balanced.

UNDER-INFLATION: Under-inflation causes a tyre to wear on the outer edges, leaving the central tread area less worn. Under inflated tyres will increase your fuel consumption.

OVER-INFLATION: Over-inflation will mean less tread is in contact with the road and the tyre will wear excessively in the centre of the tread.

POOR ALIGNMENT: Misalignment of the front wheels can cause many different wear patterns to a tyre, all of which affect the safety and handling of the car.

ILLEGAL WEAR: Tyres worn below the 1.6mm legal limit have little or no remaining tread and are extremely dangerous, especially in the wet.

IMPACT DAMAGE: Damage caused by an impact to the sidewall of the tyre will often leave a bulge indicating the area of damage or the fabric of the tyre showing through. A tyre like this is not road legal because of the potential for it to burst.

EMERGENCY BRAKING: A flat spot can be caused by emergency braking where the wheels lock and part of the tyre is held in contact with the road. Flat spots can create a judder or tremors felt through the steering. In more extreme cases, the tyre can wear right through the rubber causing it to deflate. Cars fitted with ABS are less likely to encounter this problem as the wheels are prevented from locking.

CHANGE A WHEEL

BACKGROUND KNOWLEDGE

Changing a wheel is a fairly simple job but always a mucky one because the wheels get covered in road grime and brake dust. If you're already confident at changing a wheel, remember it can be a bad idea to attempt it in certain circumstances, for instance at the side of a motorway or anywhere at night. It's far better to call out the breakdown service than take a risk.

Many new cars no longer come with full size spare wheels. Instead a 'space saver' is provided, which is a thinner wheel designed as a temporary solution to get you home or to the nearest garage. These wheels are only intended to be used for short distances of around 50 miles and at a maximum speed of 50 mph. Some cars may not have a spare wheel at all and use 'run flat' tyres which are strong enough to carry the weight of the car even with a puncture. Like a space saver, 'run flat' tyres are only designed as a temporary fix to get you home or to a nearby garage and should only be used for a short distance and at a reduced speed.

WHAT YOU'LL NEED

To change a wheel you need a jack to raise the car and wheel brace to undo the wheel nuts. If your car has alloy wheels you may also have a security 'locking wheel nut' on each wheel, which makes it more difficult for someone to steal your wheels. A locking wheel nut key is needed to remove these type of wheel nuts.

Locking wheelnut

Wheelnut key

Your car should come with all the tools required to change a wheel, often packed inside the spare wheel itself. The locking wheel nut key may also be kept here. Pack some rubber gloves along with the tool kit in case you do ever need to change a wheel.

HOW TO
CHANGE A WHEEL

If you've never changed a wheel, practice at home to boost your confidence and make sure your first attempt isn't at the roadside. Always make sure the car is on solid, flat ground and that passengers are out of the car. Finally, make sure the steering is straight, a low gear or 'PARK' is engaged and the hand brake is firmly applied.

Don't try changing a wheel at the side of a busy road, especially with your back into the road.
Call for breakdown assistance instead.

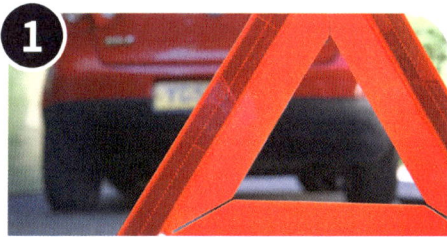

1

SAFETY FIRST

If you are by the road side turn on your hazard lights and use a warning triangle if you have one. Place the warning triangle at least 30 metres from the car.

2

APPLY HANDBRAKE

Make sure the car is switched off and apply the hand brake securely. If the car is an automatic, place it in 'Park'. Get the spare wheel, wheel brace and jack from the boot.

3

REMOVE WHEEL CAP

If you have a hubcap, remove it first. You can often use the end of the wheel brace to prise it off. If you have alloy wheels, you may need to remove the centre cap, as shown in the photo.

4

FIND JACKING POINT

Locate the jacking point under the car. This is usually a reinforced metal area. Position the jack in the correct place but don't raise the car yet. Refer to the car handbook if you're unsure.

5 LOOSEN WHEEL NUTS

Use the wheel brace to loosen the wheel nuts by half a turn. They can be very tight and you may need to apply pressure with your foot.

6 RAISE CAR

Raise the car until the tyre is no longer contacting the ground. Now remove the wheel nuts in a diagonal pattern leaving the top one for last. (Holding your foot against the bottom of the tyre may help.)

7 REMOVE WHEEL

Grip the wheel at either side and pull it away from the car. Occasionally road dirt may cause the wheel to stick. Wiggle the wheel from side to side to help release it.

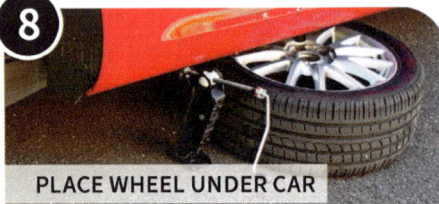

8 PLACE WHEEL UNDER CAR

Place the wheel you've just removed under the car. This will protect you and the car if it were to fall off the jack.

9 REPLACE WHEEL

Roughly line up the holes or studs on the car with the spare wheel. Once in the correct position lift it up and into place. Put all the wheel nuts back on hand tight, starting with the top one.

10 TIGHTEN WHEEL NUTS

Tighten the wheel nuts in a diagonal pattern using the wheel brace. Be careful not to use too much force that could pull the car off the jack. You can tighten them further when the car is lowered.

11 LOWER CAR

Lower the car back down gently until you can remove the jack from under the car. (Remember to move the wheel you placed under the car first!)

12 RECHECK WHEEL NUTS

Re-tighten all the wheel nuts in a diagonal pattern, being careful not to overtighten them. Check the tyre pressure at the first opportunity if it hasn't been done recently.

WINTER CHECKLIST ❄

✓ **COOLANT:** The coolant mixture is especially important in winter to protect against freezing. Coolant is generally a 50:50 mixture of water and antifreeze. If you've had to top up but only added water without antifreeze, get the coolant mixture checked at a garage.

✓ **WIPERS & WASHERS:** Check the rubber hasn't cracked or perished and the wipers aren't leaving streak marks across the screen. Test the washer jets to make sure they aren't blocked and are pointing where you want them. Most washer jets can be unblocked and repositioned with a pin.

✓ **SCREEN WASH:** Use a ready mixed winter formula or mix your own screen wash to a higher concentration. Top up every few weeks as you'll use it much faster than you realise.

✓ **LIGHTS:** Check your lights on a regular basis throughout winter as you'll be using them a lot more with fewer hours of daylight. Refer to the bulb section in the 'MOT checklist' for more information.

✓ **BATTERY & ALTERNATOR:** Flat batteries cause most breakdowns in winter; get it checked before a cold snap. A garage or motor spares store will be able to test the battery and make sure it's charging properly.

✓ **TYRE PRESSURES:** Cold temperatures will cause your tyre pressures to fall. Make regular checks, especially in very cold weather.

✓ **TYRE CONDITION:** If the tread is getting low, consider having the tyres replaced before winter. Good tread is vital for good grip in wet conditions.

✓ **ICE SCRAPER & DE-ICER:** Buy them at the start of winter and keep them in the boot. Shops can sell out very quickly when the morning frosts start to arrive! Lock de-icer is useful in severe weather for cars without remote central locking.

✓ **CLEANING:** A regular wash in winter will protect the bodywork from corrosion caused by salty gritted roads and general grime.

MOT CHECKLIST

BACKGROUND KNOWLEDGE

Your car needs an MOT every year once it's three years old. Taking the time to prepare your car for an MOT will reduce the chances of it failing for something minor such as a dead light bulb. You'll also avoid the hassle and potential cost of bringing the car back for a re-test. The next few pages cover some easy checks you can make yourself before an MOT to greatly increase the chances of your car passing.

Having your car serviced just before an MOT should pick up any faults that might cause it to fail.

LIGHTS: Over 20 percent of all MOT failures are due to lights. Use the list below to make sure you've checked all your lights. Park up close to a wall or garage door if you don't have anyone to help you check them.

Some indicator and brake light bulbs on older cars have a colour coating which starts to peel as they age. When the colour flakes off, the bulb shines white and is cause enough for a test failure. Check the colours are correct at the same time as making sure they all work. All light fittings should be secure without cracks or damage.

Headlights	Main beam & dipped
Sidelights	Front & rear
Indicators	Front, rear and side indicators
Brake lights	
Number plate	Lights only on rear number plate
Reverse lights	Not part of MOT but worth checking
Rear fog light	Front fogs not checked
Hazards	Check this separately from indicators

WHEELS & TYRES: All the tyres should be above the legal minimum tread depth of 1.6mm across ¾ of the tyre's width. There should be no damage on the tyres. Check for splits in the tread, bulges or cuts to the sidewalls. Check the tyre sizes – the front tyres must be the same size and the rear tyres must be the same size. Make sure there are no missing wheels nuts or any heavy damage to the wheels themselves. A spare wheel is not a requirement for the MOT and is not checked unless it is being used as a road wheel at the time. A 'space saver' spare fitted as a road wheel will not pass the MOT.

WINDSCREEN: Check the windscreen for chips and cracks. The car will fail the MOT for chips over 10mm in the driver's line of sight (A) (use the width of the steering wheel as a guide) and over 40mm in the area swept by the wipers (B). Any scratching that limits the drivers vision will also be a reason for a failed test.

Get small stone chips repaired as soon as possible to stop them spreading any further and costing you the price of a new windscreen.

CONTINUED:
MOT CHECKLIST

WIPERS: The wiper blades should be secure and clear the screen effectively for their entire length. Lift them up and check the rubber is not split or perished and that they are safely attached to the wiper arm.

WASHER JETS: Top up your screen wash before taking the car for it's MOT and test the jets to make sure they operate correctly. Blocked nozzles can be easily cleared with a pin.

STEERING: The steering system isn't something you'll be able to check easily apart from making sure the wheels can turn freely from lock to lock and the power steering is working correctly if you have it.

FUEL: If you car takes petrol or diesel, the fuel cap needs to lock securely in place and the seal inside the cap shouldn't be split or perished.

EXHAUST: The exhaust needs to be held on securely and not have any holes (apart from the obvious one at the end!). If your car exhaust is sounding louder than normal there's a good chance it has a hole in it. You might be able to tell by getting your ear low to the ground on the driver's side and listening carefully as you blip the accelerator (when the car is parked). If you go over a bump and the exhaust clunks on the underside of the car, the rubber mounts may be worn and in need of replacement.

HORN: The horn needs to work and be loud enough to attract the attention of pedestrians or other motorists. Musical air horns are a guaranteed fail!

MIRRORS: The mirrors need to be in place and secure, i.e. not held to the car with sticky tape and string. The glass shouldn't be cracked or smashed.

BODY: The car's bodywork must be free from heavy corrosion, not be badly damaged or have sharp edges sticking out. The front doors should work from inside and outside and the rear doors will need to work so other parts of the test can be completed such as seat belt checks. The boot and bonnet need to close securely.

BRAKES: Most checks on the braking system require specialist knowledge but there are some easy things you can test. Make sure the rubber on all the pedals isn't worn away and if your car has ABS, the warning light should go out after the car is started. The hand brake should hold the car on a hill.

NUMBER PLATES: Front and back plates need to be secured properly to the car and not cracked, faded or hidden by dirt. The letters and numbers should be standard and evenly spaced.

SEATS & BELTS: All the seat belt buckles should latch and fasten securely and lock when you give them a sharp tug. The belts need to be in good condition, not cut or badly frayed. The seats must be firmly bolted down; grab the base of each seat and try rocking it.

EMISSIONS: The best way to ensure your car passes the emissions test with ease is to have the car serviced prior to its MOT. On top of this, if your car hasn't been run in a while or is mainly used for short town journeys, take it on a longer motorway type journey where a higher engine speed is sustained for a greater length of time. This helps to clean out sooty deposits from the engine prior to the emissions test. The emissions test doesn't apply to electric vehicles, so it's one less thing to worry about if you have an EV!

WARNING LIGHTS: Your car will fail if certain dashboard warning lights are on. This includes the engine (MIL), electronic stability control (ESC), steering, airbags (SRS), anti-lock brakes (ABS) and tyre pressure monitoring systems (TPMS).